THE LONDON BAPTIST
CONFESSION
OF 1646

A Modern Version for the Church Today

"I have no doubt that our Sovereign God will use this updated version of the Confession to reform today's church for His glory, and thus increase our joy in Christ."

—CHARLES R. MOORE, JR.
Senior Pastor, First Baptist Church of Paducah, Kentucky

"For various reasons – theological, doxological, ecclesiastical and now even legal/political – churches need thorough, historic and orthodox confessions of faith. The London Confession should be the one to which Reformed Baptists look for all of these. Hopefully this modern version will help maintain and enhance its usefulness for a new generation."

—CARL TRUEMAN
Paul Woolley Professor of Church History, Westminster Theological Seminary, Pennsylvania

"With the help of the Holy Spirit and the faith and love of those before us, the good deposit continues to get passed down from generation to generation. Lord willing, this modern confession will help churches articulate their faith and guard it as others did before them."

—GREGORY BROWN
Lead Pastor, Handong International Congregation, South Korea

"In the seventeenth century, Baptist churches of Reformed convictions were not afraid to explain their faith for the benefit of fellow-believers and for others. This version of the 1646 confession, changed only in points of expression, will serve the same Christian purpose in the twenty-first century."

—DAVID BEBBINGTON
Professor of History, University of Stirling, Scotland

"In a day and age when compromise and concessions are all too prevalent, a modern rendering of this humble, yet noble, confession is needed more than ever."

—JON J. CARDWELL
Pastor of Sovereign Grace Baptist Church, Anniston, Alabama

"Creeds and confessions are an essential means to maintain, teach, and transmit the faith that was once for all delivered to the saints. Modern saints are certainly enriched by the reprint of this first Particular Baptist Confession."

—PASCAL DENAULT
Pastor, Evangelical Reformed Baptist Church of Saint-Jérôme, Québec

"One of the most classic and doctrinally rich Baptist confessions of faith has been made accessible for this and coming generations."

—CHRIS WHORTON
Pastor, Grace Christian Fellowship of Wyandotte Co., Kansas

"The first advance of Calvinistic Baptist truth in the British Isles during the tumultuous 1640s and 1650s took place on the basis of this confession of faith. I am thrilled that it is still considered of great value for use by modern congregations. May the blessing that attended its first publication likewise attend this modern rendition."

—MICHAEL A.G. HAYKIN
Professor of Church History,
The Southern Baptist Theological Seminary

"What could be better for today's church than a closer acquaintance with those great doctrines on which it rests. This new edition of the 1646 London Baptist confession, preserving that historic document for a new generation, will doubtless be of help to that end. Warmly recommended!"

—FRED G. ZASPEL
Pastor, Reformed Baptist Church, Franconia, PA, and Adjunct Professor of Theology at The Southern Baptist Theological Seminary

"My hope and prayer is that pastors and churches will use this updated confession not only as a doctrinal statement that summarizes the teaching of their churches, but they will also use it in their worship and discipleship in their churches. My heart rejoiced as I read over these glorious truths, and I hope this accessible version will help many more hearts to rejoice as well."

—PHILL HOWELL
Pastor, Embassy Church, Palatine, IL

"It is my hope that this modern version will be mightily used to help the individual Christian and the Church to walk in godliness and peace according to the New Covenant rule of Christ (Gal. 6:14-16)."

—GARY D. LONG
Faculty President Emeritus,
Providence Theological Seminary

"I am very pleased to endorse this modern version of the *London Baptist Confession of 1646*. It is greatly needed in our day."

—GEOFF VOLKER
Pastor, New Covenant Bible Fellowship, Gilbert, Arizona

THE LONDON BAPTIST
CONFESSION
OF 1646

A Modern Version for the Church Today

Edited with an Introduction
by David H. Wenkel, PhD

AMBASSADOR INTERNATIONAL
GREENVILLE, SOUTH CAROLINA & BELFAST, NORTHERN IRELAND

www.ambassador-international.com

The London Baptist Confession of 1646

A Modern Version for the Church Today

Edited with an Introduction by David H. Wenkel, PhD

© 2017 by David H. Wenkel, PhD

All rights reserved

ISBN: 978-1-62020-608-9

eISBN: 978-1-62020-681-2

Cover Design & Page Layout by Hannah Nichols
eBook Conversion by Anna Riebe Raats

AMBASSADOR INTERNATIONAL
Emerald House
411 University Ridge, Suite B14
Greenville, SC 29601, USA
www.ambassador-international.com

AMBASSADOR BOOKS
The Mount
2 Woodstock Link
Belfast, BT6 8DD, Northern Ireland, UK
www.ambassadormedia.co.uk

The colophon is a trademark of Ambassador

THE LONDON BAPTIST CONFESSION

A MODERN VERSION FOR THE CHURCH TODAY

1646

CONTENTS

Christ as Priest: His Work
Christ as Priest: His Person
Christ as King: His Work
Christ as King: His Person

Redemption
Faith
Union
Preaching
Preparation
Grace
Adoption
Justification
Sanctification
Christian Joy
Christian Suffering
Perseverance

Church and the Kingdom
Church Promises
Church Membership
Church Offices
The Duty of Pastors
The Support of Pastors
The Lord's Supper
Baptism and Immersion
Baptism and its Administration
Church Authority
Church Discipline
Church Leadership

INTRODUCTION

There are three important Baptist confessions from the Calvinistic tradition: (1) the *London Baptist Confession of 1644*, (2) the *London Baptist Confession of 1646*, and (3) the *London Baptist Confession of 1689*. This modern version of the *London Baptist Confession of 1646* (hereafter "Confession" unless otherwise noted) is designed for use in the local church today. It was edited for use as a confession (or statement of faith) for Baptist churches in the Reformed tradition.

The Confession was originally drawn up and signed in 1646 by seven churches in London. This was a "corrected and enlarged" edition of the first confession published in 1644. The title of the original Confession of 1646 was: "A Confession of Faith of Seven Congregations or Churches of Christ in London, Which are Commonly (But Unjustly) Called Anabaptists." A copy of the original Confession is widely available on the internet and is published in standard reference books such as *Baptist Confessions of Faith* edited by W.L. Lumpkin and B.J. Leonard (2011). The modern version presented here is based on the edition printed by Matthew Simmons and John Hancock in Popes-head Alley, London, 1646. This edition is available online from The Angus Library and Archive at Regent's Park College, University of Oxford.

CHALLENGING ASPECTS OF THE CONFESSION

Local churches interested in using the Confession today should first consider these four challenges.

The first challenge is its omission of statements on the doctrine of Scripture that subsequent debates through the centuries now require. The Confession addresses the doctrine of Scripture, but this doctrine is sometimes assumed rather than explained. The Confession celebrates the truthfulness and excellence of Scripture, yet nowhere does it identify the Bible as inerrant or even inspired. However, the concept of the inspiration of Scripture is certainly present even if the term is not used. There are references to the nature of faith in relation to God's "revealed or written word" (article 22), the centrality of preaching the word of God (article 44), and the concept of the authority of the Old and New Testament (article 49), etc. This issue might be addressed by supplementing the Confession with the Chicago Statement on Biblical Inerrancy.

Second, the doctrine of the Holy Spirit, his person and work, is not singularly addressed in any article. Like the doctrine of Scripture, a close reading of the articles will demonstrate that the doctrine of the Holy Spirit is found in many places. Rather than having a dedicated article, the doctrine of the person and work of the Holy Spirit is woven throughout. He is referenced at least fourteen times and is given specific attention in articles 1 and 2 in relation to the doctrine of God. The doctrine of the Holy Spirit is actually robust when all of the statements in the Confession are considered together.

Third, the Confession does not address human sexuality and the roles of men and women in marriage. The requirement for elders or pastors to be men is clearly stated in article 44; however, the topic of human sexuality and the role of women in the church was not a major issue at the time this Confession was originally written. Today, the cultural and legal context of the world requires that churches have a clear written statement about these matters. This omission might be addressed by adopting the Danver's Statement by the Council on Biblical Manhood and Womanhood.

Fourth, the Confession is rather long compared to contemporary denominational statements of faith. The length of any confession is a double-edged sword. If a confession is too detailed, it can become impractical for use in a local church with people who have varying levels of theological training. But if a confession is too short, it can lead to division, confusion, and deviant doctrine. For example, some churches may be uncomfortable with the lack of detail in this Confession regarding the "end times." However, some Christians may view this brevity as an opportunity for Christian unity.

CONTEXTUALIZING THE CONFESSION

The goal of this modern version is to maintain the meaning and message of the original Confession while presenting it in a new way for today's readers in the local church. Therefore, this version does not introduce any substantial changes to the text. The changes have been minimal. The following characteristics have remained the same: the general style of English, the number of articles, the order of the articles, and the concluding Bible verse with prayer (the benediction).

Statements of faith, or Confessions, should be relatively accessible to those considering church membership. As such, core Christian doctrines should be made understandable even for new Christians. This requires a degree of contextualization –- stripping away some historical elements of the past and adding contemporary elements so that the text can be understood by a wide range of people. The primary goal of this modern version is to expand this Confession's relevance for the church today without losing its message and doctrine.

This modern version of the Confession has elements that reflect a spectrum of contextualization. Some aspects were changed, while others remain untouched. Some aspects of the Confession's historical character have been removed: the original preface, signatures, a special note on obeying the King and Parliament after article 48, and the conclusion. While these items remain important for historians and theologians, they would prove unhelpful or distracting to average church members today.

This modern version of the Confession reflects the desire of the pastors and churches who first wrote it. They were not afraid to update and change their first edition, the London Baptist Confession of 1644. The cover page of the London Baptist Confession of 1646 indicates in bold type that it is a "second impression – corrected and enlarged." This modern version shares the same perspective: confessions need to be updated.

It is sometimes necessary to introduce changes for several reasons. One simple but important reason is that, like all languages, English has changed and will continue to change. All languages change over time, and English is no exception. Perhaps in another three-hundred years, this modern version of the Confession will need to be updated again to reflect future changes to the English language. The Confession includes seven types of changes:

(1) Updates. Words like "hath," "doth," "befalls," and "saith" and words with antiquated endings like "giveth" have been updated to modern equivalents. Some words that were previously separated have been joined (e.g. for evermore is now "forevermore"). British spellings of words such as "honour" and "saviour" have been preserved in order to reflect the British heritage of the Confession. Following the pattern of the original, this version has not capitalized every pronoun for God.

(2) Interpretations. A few changes are better labeled "interpretations" rather than simply updates. For example, the word "Prophecie" in article 45 has been changed to "preach" in order to reflect its meaning.

(3) Phraseology. Phrases have been updated to reflect a modern English idiom (e.g. "to wit" meaning "that is to say"). At other times, commas and other punctuation have been inserted to add clarity to long and difficult sentences. In some instances, comparisons of the KJV with modern bible versions such as the ESV, NIV, and NET provide parallels with older English idioms (e.g. "made nigh" was changed to "brought close").

(4) Headings. New headings have been added to simplify and clarify the content of each article. Each header now begins with a word or phrase that identifies it as a doctrine. The ending of the Confession has been labeled a "benediction."

(5) Sections. Another new characteristic of this modern version of the London Baptist Confession of 1646 is the inclusion of section headers such as "The Doctrine of God" and "The Doctrine of Christ." The Confession contains fifty-two articles, and this length is somewhat unwieldy for today's readers. The section headers are intended to provide readers with an easy way to understand the content and to locate articles.

(6) Scripture References. The original Confession had numerous biblical proof-texts in the footnotes and margins. This was done to demonstrate that these articles reflect the truth of Scripture. The order of the proof-texts generally follows the order of the original. It should be possible for a church to adopt this Confession without adopting all of the individual decisions about various supporting Bible verses. In a few instances, proof-texts have been changed because it is evident there was a mistake by the authors or printer.

Ultimately, the Scripture is the foundation for our faith, and the strength of any confession is its faithfulness to it.

(7) Culture. This version attempts to keep some elements of the historical British character of this Confession while making it suitable for other English-speaking countries. Again, the goal of this modern version is to expand its relevance without sacrificing its content and message.

To summarize: this modern version seeks to strike a balance that will preserve the meaning and message of the articles while contextualizing it for today's readers in the local church.

SECTION I: THE DOCTRINE OF GOD

GOD'S ATTRIBUTES

The Lord our God is but one God, whose subsistence is in himself; whose essence cannot be comprehended by any but himself; who only has immortality, dwelling in unapproachable light; who is in himself most holy, every way infinite in greatness, wisdom, power, and love; merciful and gracious, long-suffering and abundant in goodness and truth, who gives being, moving, and preservation to all creatures.

1 Corinthians 8:6; Isaiah 44:6, 46:9; Exodus 3:14; 1 Timothy 6:16; Isaiah 43:15; Psalm 147:5; Deuteronomy 32:3; Job 36:5; Jeremiah 10:12; Exodus 34:6-7; Acts 17:28; Romans 11:36

GOD'S PERSONS

In this divine and infinite Being, there is the Father, the Word, and the Holy Spirit, each having the whole divine essence, yet the essence undivided; all infinite and without any beginning; therefore, but one God, who is not to be divided in nature and being, but distinguished by several peculiar relative properties.

1 Corinthians 1:3; John 1:1, 15:26; Exodus 3:14; 1 Corinthians 8:6

GOD'S DECREES

God has decreed in himself before the world was, concerning all things, whether necessary, accidental, or voluntary, with all the circumstances of them, to work, dispose, and bring about all things, according to the counsel of his own will, to his glory: (yet without being the author of sin, or having fellowship with any therein) in which appears his wisdom in disposing all things, his unchangeableness, power, and faithfulness in accomplishing his decree, and God has, before the foundation of the world, foreordained some people to eternal life, through Jesus Christ, to the praise and glory of his grace; leaving the rest in their sin to their just condemnation, to the praise of his justice.

Isaiah 46:10; Ephesians 1:11; Romans 11:33; Psalm 115:3, 135:6; Psalm 33:15; 1 Samuel 10:9-26; Proverbs 21:6; Exodus 21:13; Proverbs 16:33; Psalm 144; Isaiah 45:7; Jeremiah 14:22; Matthew 6:28, 30; Colossians 1:16-17; Numbers 23:19-20; Romans 3:4; Jeremiah 10:10; Ephesians 1:4-5; Jude 4, 6; Proverbs 16:4

GOD'S CREATION

In the beginning, God made all things very good. He created man after his own image and filled him with all suitable perfection of nature, and made him free from all sin, but he did not live with this honor for very long. Satan, using the subtlety of the serpent, seduced first Eve, then by her, seduced Adam who, without any compulsion in eating the forbidden fruit, transgressed the command of God and fell, whereby death came upon all his posterity, who now are conceived in sin, and by nature the children of wrath, the servants of sin, the subjects of death, and other miseries in this world and forever, unless the Lord Jesus Christ set them free.

Genesis 1:1; Colossians 1:16; Isaiah 45:12; 1 Corinthians 15:45-46; Ecclesiastes 7:29; Genesis 3:1, 4:5; 2 Corinthians 11:3; Galatians 3:22; Romans 5:12, 18-19, 6:22; Ephesians 2:3

GOD'S PROVIDENCE

God, in his infinite power and wisdom, does dispose all things to the end for which they were created, that neither good nor evil occurs by chance or without his providence, and that whatsoever happens to the elect is by his appointment, for his glory, and for their good.

Job 38:11; Isaiah 46:10-11; Ecclesiastes 3:14; Matthew 10:29-30; Exodus 21:13; Proverbs 16:33; Romans 8:28

GOD'S LOVE

All the elect, being loved of God with an everlasting love, are redeemed, brought to life, and saved, not by themselves, nor their own works lest anyone should boast, but only and wholly by God, of his free grace and mercy through Jesus Christ, who is made unto us by God, wisdom, righteousness, sanctification, and redemption, and all in all, so that anyone who rejoices might rejoice in the Lord.

Jeremiah 31:3; Ephesians 1:3-7, 2:4-9; 1 Thessalonians 5:9; Acts 13:38; 2 Corinthians 5:21; Jeremiah 9:23-24; 1 Corinthians 1:30-32; Jeremiah 23:6

GOD'S SALVATION

And this is life eternal, that we might know him, the only true God, and Jesus Christ, whom he has sent. And on the contrary, the Lord will render vengeance in flaming fire to them who do not know God and do not obey the Gospel of Jesus Christ.

John 17:3; Hebrews 5:9; 1 Thessalonians 1:8; John 6:36

GOD'S WORSHIP

The rule of this knowledge, faith, and obedience, concerning the worship of God, in which is contained the whole duty of mankind, is (not people's laws, or unwritten traditions) only the Word of God contained in the holy Scriptures, in which is plainly recorded whatsoever is needful for us to know, believe, and practice, which are the only rule of holiness and obedience for all saints, at all times, in all places to be observed.

Colossians 2:23; Matthew 15:9; Job 5:39; 2 Timothy 3:15-17; Isaiah 8:20; Galatians 1:8-9; Acts 3:22-23

SECTION II: THE DOCTRINE OF CHRIST

CHRIST AS INCARNATE

The Lord Jesus Christ, of whom Moses and the prophets wrote and the apostles preached, is the Son of God, the brightness of his glory, by whom the world was made, and he upholds and governs all things that he has made; who also, when the fullness of time was come, was made of a woman who was of the tribe of Judah and of the seed of Abraham and David; that is to say, of the virgin Mary, the Holy Spirit coming down upon her, and the power of the Most High overshadowing her. He was tempted as we are, yet without sin.

Genesis 3:15, 22:18, 49:10; Daniel 7:13, 9:24-26; Proverbs 8:23; John 1:1-3; Hebrews 1:8; Galatians 4:4; Hebrews 7:14; Revelation 5:5; Genesis 49:9-10; Romans 1:3, 9:5; Matthew 1:16; Luke 3:23-26; Hebrews 2:16; Isaiah 53:3-5; Hebrews 4:15

CHRIST AS COVENANTED

Jesus Christ is made the Mediator of the new and everlasting covenant of grace between God and man, ever to be perfectly and fully the Prophet, Priest, and King of the Church of God forevermore.

1 Timothy 2:5; Hebrews 9:15; John 14:6; Isaiah 9:6-7

CHRIST AS ANOINTED

Unto this office he was appointed by God from everlasting, and in respect of his manhood, he was from the womb called, separated, and anointed most fully and abundantly with all gifts necessary for God, having without measure, poured out his Spirit upon him.

Proverbs 8:23; Isaiah 42:6, 49:1, 6; Isaiah 11:2-5, 61:1-2, Luke 4:17, 22; John 1:14, 16, 3:34

CHRIST AS CALLED

Concerning his mediatorship, the Scripture holds forth Christ's call to his office: For none takes this honour upon him but he that is called of God, as was Aaron, it being an action of God; whereby, a special promise being made, he ordains his Son to this office; which promise is, that Christ should be made a sacrifice for sin, that he should see his seed and prolong his days, that the pleasure of the Lord shall prosper in his hand, all of mere free and absolute grace towards God's elect, and without any condition foreseen in them to procure it.

Hebrews 5:4-6; Isaiah 53:10-11; John 3:16; Romans 8:32

CHRIST AS UNIQUE

This office to be Mediator, to be Prophet, Priest, and King of the church of God, is so proper to Christ that it can neither in whole, nor any part thereof be transferred from him to any other.

1 Timothy 2:5; Hebrews 7:24; Daniel 7:14; Acts 4:12; Luke 1:33; John 14:6

CHRIST AS THREE-FOLD

This office, to which Christ is called, is threefold as a Prophet, Priest, and King. This number and order of offices is necessary because, in respect of our ignorance, we stand in need of his prophetic office. And in respect of our great alienation from God, we need his priestly office to reconcile us, and in respect of our opposition and utter inability to return to God, we need his kingly office to convince, subdue, draw, uphold, and preserve us to his heavenly kingdom.

Deuteronomy 18:15, Acts 3:22-23; Hebrews 3:1, 4:14-15; Psalm 2:6; 2 Corinthians 5:20; Acts 26:18; Colossians 1:21; John 16:8; Psalm 110:3; Song of Songs 1:4; John 6:44; Philippians 4:13; 2 Timothy 4:18

CHRIST AS PROPHET: HIS WORK

Concerning the prophecy of Christ, it is that whereby he has revealed the will of God, whatsoever is needful for his servants to know and obey, and therefore, he is called not only a Prophet, Healer, the Apostle of our profession, and the Messenger of the covenant, but also, the very Wisdom of God, in whom are hidden all the treasures of wisdom and knowledge, who forever continues revealing the same truth of the gospel to his people.

John 1:18, 12:49-50, 17:8; Deuteronomy 18:15; Matthew 23:10; Hebrews 3:1; Malachi 3:1; 1 Corinthians 1:24; Colossians 2:3

CHRIST AS PROPHET: HIS PERSON

That he might be a Prophet in every way complete, it was necessary he should be God and also, that he should be man; for unless he had been God, he could never have perfectly understood the will of God, and unless he had been man, he could not suitably have unfolded it in his own person to others.

John 1:18; Acts 3:22, with Deuteronomy 18:15; Hebrews 1:1

SPECIAL NOTE: CHRIST'S DIVINITY

That Jesus Christ is God is wonderfully and clearly expressed in the Scriptures. He is called the mighty God, which Word was God, Christ who is God over all, God manifested in the flesh, and the same is very God. He is the first, he gives being to all things, and without him was nothing made. He forgives sins, is before Abraham, and he was, and is, and ever will be the same. He is always with those that are his, to the end of the world, which could not be said of Jesus Christ if he were not God. And to the Son, he says: "your throne, O God, is forever and ever." Christ is not only perfectly God, but also, perfectly man. He was made of a woman who was made of the seed of David, a physical descendant of David, Jesse, and Judah, in that the children were partakers of flesh and blood, he himself likewise took part with them. He took not on himself the nature of angels but the seed of Abraham so that we are bone of his bone and flesh of his flesh. So that he that sanctifies and they that are sanctified are all of one.

John 1:18; Acts 3:22; Deuteronomy 18:15; Hebrews 1:1; Isaiah 9:6; John 1:1; Romans 9:5; 1 Timothy 3:16; 1 John 5:20; Revelation 1:8; John 1:3; Matthew 9:6; John 8:58;

*Hebrews 13:8; Matthew 28:20; Hebrews 1:8; John 1:18; Acts 20:28; Romans 1:3;
Acts 2:30; Hebrews 2:16; Ephesians 5:30; Hebrews 2:11; Acts 3:22; Deuteronomy 18:15;
Hebrews 1:1*

CHRIST AS PRIEST: HIS WORK

Concerning his priesthood, Christ, having sanctified himself, has appeared once to put away sin by that one offering of himself, a sacrifice for sin. He has fully finished and suffered all things God required for the salvation of his elect and removed all rites and shadows. He is now entered within the veil, into the Holy of Holies, which is the presence of God. He makes his people a spiritual house, a holy priesthood, to offer up spiritual sacrifices acceptable to God through him. Neither does the Father accept, nor does Christ offer to the Father, any other worship or worshippers.

*John 17:19; Hebrews 5:7-10; Romans 5:19; Ephesians 5:2; Colossians 1:20; Ephesians 2:14-16;
Romans 8:32; Hebrews 9:24 and 8:1, 1 Peter 2:5; John 4:23-24*

CHRIST AS PRIEST: HIS PERSON

This priesthood was not legal or temporary, but according to the order of Melchizedek, is stable and perfect, not for a time, but forever. This is suitable to Jesus Christ, as is to him that ever lives. Christ was the Priest, the sacrifice, and the altar. He was a Priest according to both natures. He was a sacrifice according to his human nature, and for this reason, in scripture, it is attributed to his body and to his blood. The effectualness of this sacrifice also depended upon his divine nature; therefore, it is called the blood of God. He was the altar according to his divine nature, it belonging to the altar to sanctify that which is offered upon it, and so, it ought to be of greater dignity than the Sacrifice itself.

Hebrews 7:17; Hebrews 7:16, 18, 20-21, 24-25; Hebrews 5:6, 10:10; 1 Peter 1:18-19; Colossians 1:20, 22; Hebrews 9:13; Acts 20:28; Hebrews 9:14, 13:10, 12, 15; Matthew 23:17; John 17:19

CHRIST AS KING: HIS WORK

Concerning his kingly office, Christ being risen from the dead, ascended into heaven, and having all power in heaven and earth, he spiritually governs his church and exercises his power over all angels and people, both good and bad, to the preservation and salvation of the elect and to the over-ruling and destruction of his enemies. By this kingly power, he applies the benefits, virtues, and fruits of his prophecy and priesthood to his elect. He subdues their sins, preserving and strengthening them in all their conflicts against Satan, the world, and the flesh, keeping their hearts in faith and filial fear by his Spirit. By this, his mighty power, he rules the vessels of wrath by using, limiting, and restraining them as it seems good to his infinite wisdom.

1 Corinthians 15:4; 1 Peter 3:21-22; Matthew 28:18-19; Luke 24:51; Acts 1:2 and 5:30-31; John 20:17; Romans 14:9; John 5:26-27; Romans 5:6-8, 14, 17; Galatians 5:22-23; Mark 1:27; Hebrews 1:14; John 16:15; Job 1:8, 2:6; Romans 9:21,17-18; Ephesians 4:17-18; 2 Peter 2:9

CHRIST AS KING: HIS PERSON

This, his kingly power, shall be more fully manifest when he shall come in glory to reign among his saints, and he shall put down all rule and authority under his feet that the glory of the Father may be perfectly manifested in his Son and the glory of the Father and the Son in all his members.

1 Corinthians 15:24, 28; Hebrews 9:28; 2 Thessalonians 1:9-10; 1 Thessalonians 4:15-17; John 17:21, 26

SECTION III: THE DOCTRINE
OF SALVATION

REDEMPTION

Jesus Christ, by his death, did purchase salvation for the elect that God gave unto him. These elect have only interest in him and fellowship with him. For these he makes intercession to his father in the behalf of, and unto them alone God does, by his Spirit, apply this redemption as the free gift of eternal life is given to them and none else.

Ephesians 1:14; Hebrews 5:9; Matthew 1:21; John 17:6; Hebrews 7:25; 1 Corinthians 2:12; Romans 8:29-30; 1 John 5:12; John 15:13; John 3:16

FAITH

Faith is the gift of God wrought in the hearts of the elect by the Spirit of God. Through faith, the elect come to know and believe the truth of the Scriptures, the excellence of them above all other writings, all things in the world as they hold forth the glory of God in all his attributes, the excellency of Christ in his nature and offices, and of the power and fullness of the Spirit in its workings and operations. They are, therefore, enabled to cast their souls upon this truth thus believed.

Ephesians 2:8; John 6:29, 4:10; Philippians 1:29; Galatians 5:22; John 17:17; Hebrews 4:11-12; John 6:63

UNION

All those that have this precious faith wrought in them by the Spirit can never finally nor totally fall away because the gifts of God are without repentance. He still creates and nourishes in them faith, repentance, love, joy, hope, and all the graces of the Spirit into immortality, and though many storms and floods arise, they shall never be able to take them off that foundation and rock which, by faith, they are fastened upon. Notwithstanding unbelief and the temptations of Satan, the sensible sight of this light and love may be clouded and overwhelmed for a time; however, God is still the same, and they shall be sure to be kept by the power of God unto salvation where they shall enjoy their purchased possession, they being engraven upon the palms of his hands and their names having been written in the book of life from all eternity.

Matthew 7:24-25; John 13:10; John 10:28-29; 1 Peter 1:4-6; Isaiah 49:13-16

PREACHING

Faith is ordinarily begotten by the preaching of the gospel or word of Christ. Without respect to any power or agency in the creature, but it being wholly passive and dead in trespasses and sins, does believe and is converted by no less power than that which raised Christ from the dead.

Romans 10:17; 1 Corinthians 1:21; Romans 9:16; Ezekiel 16:6; Romans 3:12; Romans 1:16; Ephesians 1:19; Colossians 2:12

PREPARATION

The preaching of the gospel to the conversion of sinners is absolutely free. In no way does it require as absolutely necessary any qualifications, preparations, terrors of the law, or preceding ministry of the law, but only and alone the naked soul, a sinner and ungodly, to receive Christ crucified, dead, buried, and risen again. He, who is made a Prince and a Saviour for such sinners as through the gospel, shall be brought to believe on him.

John 3:14-15, 1:12; Isaiah 55:1; John 7:37; 1 Timothy 1:15; Romans 4:5, 5:8; Acts 5:30-31, 2:36; 1 Corinthians 1:22, 24

GRACE

The same power that converts to faith in Christ also carries on the soul through all duties, temptations, conflicts, and sufferings, and whatsoever a believer is, it is by grace, and is carried on in all obedience and temptations by the same.

1 Peter 1:5; 2 Corinthians 12:9; 1 Corinthians 15:10; Philippians 2:12-13; John 15:5; Galatians 2:19-20

ADOPTION

All believers are united by Christ to God, and by this union, God is one with them and they are one with him, and all believers are the sons of God and joint heirs with Christ, and to them belong all the promises of this life and that which is to come.

1 Thessalonians 1:1; John 17:21 and 20:17; Hebrews 2:11; 1 John 4:16; Galatians 2:19-20

JUSTIFICATION

Those that have union with Christ are justified from all their sins by the blood of Christ. This justification is a gracious and full acquaintance of a guilty sinner from all sin, by God, through the satisfaction that Christ has made by his death for all their sins. This is applied through faith.

1 John 1:7; Hebrews 10:14, 9:26; 2 Corinthians 5:19; Romans 3:24; Acts 13:38-39; Romans 5:1, 3:25, 30

SANCTIFICATION

All believers are a holy and sanctified people. This sanctification is a spiritual grace of the new covenant and an effect of the love of God manifested in the soul, whereby, the believer presses after a heavenly and evangelical obedience to all the commands which Christ, as head and king in his new covenant, has prescribed to them.

1 Corinthians 1:2; 1 Peter 2:9; Ephesians 1:4; 1 John 4:16; Matthew 28:20

CHRISTIAN JOY

All believers, through the knowledge of that justification of life given by the Father and brought forth by the blood of Christ, have, as their great privilege of the new covenant, peace with God and reconciliation, whereby, they that were far away are brought near through that blood and have peace passing all understanding. Indeed, joy in God through our Lord Jesus Christ, by whom we have received the atonement.

2 Corinthians 5:19; Romans 5:9-10; Isaiah 54:10, 26:12; Ephesians 2:13-14; Philippians 4:7; Romans 5:10-11

CHRISTIAN SUFFERING

All believers, in the time of this life, are in a continual warfare and combat against sin, self, the world, and the devil. All believers are liable to all manner of afflictions, tribulations, and persecutions, being predestinated and appointed thereunto. And whatever the saints possess or enjoy of God spiritually are by faith, and outward and temporal things are lawfully enjoyed by a civil right by them who have no faith.

Romans 7:23-24; Ephesians 6:10-13; Hebrews 2:9-10; 2 Timothy 3:12; Romans 8:29; 1 Thessalonians 3:3; Galatians 2:19-20; 2 Corinthians 5:7; Deuteronomy 2:5

PERSEVERANCE

The only strength, by which the saints are enabled to encounter with all oppositions and trials, is only by Jesus Christ, who is the Captain of their salvation. Being made perfect through sufferings, he has engaged his faithfulness and strength to assist them in all their afflictions, to uphold them in all their temptations, and to preserve them by his power to his everlasting kingdom.

John 16:33; John 15:5; Philippians 4:11; Hebrews 2:9-10; 2 Timothy 4:18

SECTION IV: THE DOCTRINE
OF THE CHURCH

CHURCH AND THE KINGDOM

Jesus Christ has here on earth a spiritual kingdom, which is his church, whom he has purchased and redeemed to himself as a peculiar inheritance. His church is a company of visible saints, who are called and separated from the world by the Word and Spirit of God, to the visible profession of the faith of the gospel, being baptized into that faith and joined to the Lord and to each other, by mutual agreement in the practical enjoyment of the ordinances commanded by Christ their Head and King.

2 Thessalonians 1:5; 1 Corinthians 1:2; Ephesians 1:1; Acts 2:37, 10:37, 19:8-9, 26:18; 2 Corinthians 6:17; Revelation 18:4; Romans 1:7, 10:10; Matthew 11:11, 28:19-20; Acts 2:42, 9:26; 1 Peter 2:5

CHURCH PROMISES

To this church, he has made his promises and given the signs of his covenant, presence, acceptance, love, blessings, and protection. Here are the fountains and springs of his heavenly graces flowing forth to refresh and strengthen them.

Matthew 28:18-20; 1 Corinthians 11:24 and 3:21; 2 Corinthians 6:18; Romans 9:4-5; Galatians 3:8-9; Romans chpts. 3, 7, 10; Ezekiel 47:2

CHURCH MEMBERSHIP

The duty of all believers is to join Christ's church and to serve him in it, especially by giving what is needful to others. And all his servants of all estates are to acknowledge him to be their Prophet, Priest, and King. They are called toward him, to be enrolled among his household servants, to present their bodies and souls, and to bring their gifts, which God has given them, to be under his heavenly conduct and government. They are to lead their lives in this walled sheepfold and watered garden and have communion here, with his saints, that they may be assured that they are made fit to be partakers of their inheritance in the kingdom of God. They should supply each other's needs, inward and outward, (and although each person has a property in their own estate, yet they are to supply each other's needs, according as their necessities shall require, that the name of Jesus Christ may not be blasphemed through the necessity of any of the church) and being come, they are here by himself, to be bestowed in their several order, due place, and peculiar use. Being fitly compacted and knit together, according to the effectual working of every part, to the edifying of itself in love.

Acts 2:41, 47; Isaiah 4:3; 1 Corinthians 12:6-7, 12, 18; Ezekiel 20:40, chpt. 37; Song of Songs 4:12; Ephesians 2:19; Romans 12:4-6; Colossians 1:12, 2:5-6, 19; Acts 20:32; Acts 4:4; Acts 2:44-45 and 4:34-35, 5:4; Luke 14:26; 1 Timothy 6:1; Ephesians 4:16

CHURCH OFFICES

Being thus joined, every church has power, given them from Christ for their well-being, to choose among themselves qualified persons for elders and deacons. Thus, being qualified, according to the word, as those which Christ has appointed in the New Testament for the feeding, governing, serving, and building up of his church, and so that none have any power to impose on them or any other.

Acts 1:23, 26, 6:3, 15:22, 25; Romans 12:7-8; 1 Timothy 3:2, 6-8; 1 Corinthians 12:8, 28; Hebrews 13:7, 17; 1 Peter 5:1-3; 1 Peter 4:15

THE DUTY OF PASTORS

That the ministers lawfully called, as mentioned above, ought to continue in their calling and place, according to God's ordinance, by carefully feeding the flock of God committed to them, not for shameful profit, but eagerly.

Hebrews 5:4; John 10:3-4; Acts 20:28-29; Romans 12:7-8; Hebrews 13:7, 17; 1 Peter 5:1-3

THE SUPPORT OF PASTORS

The ministers of Christ ought to have whatsoever they shall need supplied freely by the church. According to Christ's ordinance, they that preach the gospel should live of the gospel by the law of Christ.

1 Corinthians 9:7, 14; Galatians 6:6; 1 Thessalonians 5:13; Philippians 4:15-16; 2 Corinthians 10:4; 1 Timothy 1:9; Psalm 110:3

THE LORD'S SUPPER

Baptism is an ordinance of the New Testament, given by Christ, to be dispensed upon persons professing faith or that are made disciples. Upon profession of faith, they ought to be baptized and after to partake of the Lord's Supper.

Matthew 28:18-19; John 4:1; Mark 16:15-16; Acts 2:37-38, 8:36-38 and 18:8

BAPTISM AND IMMERSION

The mode and picture of baptism: the way and manner of dispensing this ordinance is dipping or plunging the body underwater. Immersion, being a sign, must answer the thing signified, which is, the interest the saints have in the death, burial, and resurrection of Christ. And as certainly as the body is buried under water and raised again, so certainly shall the bodies of the saints be raised, by the power of Christ, in the day of the resurrection to reign with Christ. The Greek word *Baptizo* signifies to dip or plunge (yet so as convenient garments be both upon the administrator and subject with all modesty).

Matthew 3:6, 16; Mark 1:5, 9; John 3:23; Acts 8:38; Revelation 1:5, 7:14, with Hebrews 10:22; Romans 6:3-6; 1 Corinthians 15:28-29

BAPTISM AND ITS ADMINISTRATION

The person designed by Christ to dispense baptism, the scripture holds forth, is to be a disciple; it being nowhere tied to a particular church officer or person extraordinarily sent; the commission commanding the administration, being given to them considered as disciples, being men able to preach the gospel.

Isaiah 8:16; Ephesians 3:7; Matthew 28:19; John 4:2; Acts 20:7, 11:20; 1 Corinthians 10:16-17, 11:24; Romans 16:2; Matthew 18:17

CHURCH AUTHORITY

Christ has likewise given power to his church to receive in and cast out any member that deserves it, and this power is given to every congregation and not to one particular person, neither member or officer, but in relation to the whole body in reference to their faith and fellowship.

1 Corinthians 5:4, 11-13; 6:2-3; 2 Corinthians 2:6-7

CHURCH DISCIPLINE

And every particular member of each church, no matter how excellent, great, or learned, is subject to this censure and judgment, and that the church ought not without great care, tenderness, and due advice, but by the rule of faith, to proceed against her members.

Matthew 18:16-18; Acts 11:2-3; 1 Timothy 5:19-21; Colossians 4:17; Acts 15:1-3

CHURCH LEADERSHIP

Christ, for the keeping of this church in holy and orderly communion, places some special men over the church that, by their office, are to govern, oversee, visit, and watch. Likewise, for the better keeping of the church in all places, by the members, he has given authority and laid duty upon all to watch over one another.

Acts 20:27-28; Hebrews 13:17, 27; Matthew 24:45; 1 Thessalonians 5:12-14; Jude 3, 20; Hebrews 10:34-35, 12:15

CHURCH GIFTS

Also, such to whom God has given gifts in the church they may and ought to preach according to their proportion of faith, and they should teach publicly the word of God for the edification, exhortation, and comfort of the church.

1 Corinthians 14:3; Romans 12:6; 1 Peter 4:10-11; 1 Corinthians 12:7; 1 Thessalonians 5:19-20

CHURCH PROCEDURE

Thus, being rightly gathered and continuing in the obedience of the gospel of Christ, no one should separate for faults and corruptions (for as long as the church consists of people subject to failings there will be difference in the true constituted church) until they have, in due order and tenderness, sought to make amends.

Revelation 2 and 3; Acts 15:12; 1 Corinthians 1:10; Hebrews 10:25; Jude 19; Revelation 2:20, 23, 24; Acts 15:1-2; Romans 14:1, 15:1-3

CHURCH COOPERATION

Although the particular congregations be distinct and several bodies, everyone is like a compact and knit city within itself, yet are they all to walk by one rule of truth. They (by all means convenient) are to have the counsel and help of one another, if necessity requires it, as members of one body, in the common faith, under Christ their head.

1 Corinthians 4:17, 14:33, 36, 16:1; Psalm 122:3; Ephesians 2:12, 19, with Revelation 21; 1 Timothy 3:15, 6:13-14; 1 Corinthians 4:17; Acts 15:2-3; Song of Songs 8:8-9

SECTION V: THE DOCTRINE
OF CIVIL GOVERNMENT

GOD AND CIVIL GOVERNMENT

Civil government is an ordinance of God set up by him for the punishment of evildoers and for the praise of them that do well, and that in all lawful things, commanded by them, subjection ought to be given by us in the Lord, not only for wrath, but also for conscience's sake, and we are to make supplications and prayers for kings and all who are in authority so that under them, we may live a quiet and peaceable life in all godliness and honesty.

Romans 13:1-4; 1 Peter 2:13-14; 1 Timothy 2:1-3

OBEDIENCE AND CIVIL GOVERNMENT

But in case we find the government does not favour us in these things, we dare not suspend our practice because we believe we ought to go on in obedience to Christ, in professing the faith which was once delivered to the saints (which faith is declared in the Holy Scriptures), and this our Confession of Faith apart of them. We are to witness to the truth of the Old and New Testament unto the death, if necessity require, in the midst of all trials and afflictions, as his saints of old have done, not accounting our goods, lands, wives, children, fathers, mothers, brothers, sisters, yes, and our own lives, as dear unto us, so we may finish our course with joy, remembering always that we ought to obey God rather than people. He will, when we have finished our course and kept the faith, give us the crown of righteousness. To him we must give an account of all our actions and no person being able to discharge us of the same.

Acts 2:40-41, 4:19, 5:28-29, 41, 20:23; 1 Thessalonians 3:3; Philippians 1:28-29;
Daniel 3:16-17, 6:7, 10, 22-23; 1 Timothy 6:13-15; Romans 12:1, 8; 1 Corinthians 14:37;
Revelation 2:20; 2 Timothy 4:6-8

EMPLOYMENT AND CIVIL GOVERNMENT

A Christian may be a government employee and take an oath. It is lawful for a Christian to be a magistrate or civil officer, and also, it is lawful to take an oath as long as it is in truth, in judgment, and in righteousness for confirmation of truth and the ending of all strife. It is by rash and vain oaths that the Lord is provoked and this land mourns.

Acts 8:38, 10:1-2, 35, 44; Romans 16:23; Deuteronomy 6:13; Romans 1:9;
2 Corinthians 10:11; Jeremiah 4:2; Hebrews 6:16

CHRISTIAN DUTY TO ALL PEOPLE

We are to give unto all people whatsoever is their due as their place, age, and estate requires, and so that we defraud no person of anything, but to do unto all people as we would they should do unto us.

1 Thessalonians 4:6; Romans 13:5-7; Matthew 22:21; Titus 3; 1 Peter 2:15, 17, 5:5

SECTION VI: THE DOCTRINE OF THE END

THE RESURRECTION

There shall be a resurrection of the dead, both the just and unjust, and everyone shall give an account of himself to God so that everyone may receive what is due for things done, while in the body, whether it be good or bad.

Acts 24:15; 2 Corinthians 5:10; Romans 14:12

BENEDICTION

Let not the downtrodden turn back in shame;

   let the poor and needy praise your name.

Arise, O God, defend your cause;

   remember how the foolish scoff at you all the day!

(Psalm 74:21-22, ESV)

Come, Lord Jesus, come quickly.

For more information about
David H. Wenkel
and
The London Baptist Confession of 1646
A Modern Version for the Church Today
please contact:

www.davidwenkel.com
www.reformedbaptistconfession.org
dwenkel@ymail.com

For more information about
AMBASSADOR INTERNATIONAL
please visit:

www.ambassador-international.com
@AmbassadorIntl
www.facebook.com/AmbassadorIntl